# GRIEF & OTHER ANIMALS

# GRIEF & OTHER ANIMALS

Poems by
**Patty Paine**

Accents Publishing • Lexington, Kentucky • 2015

Copyright © 2015 by Patty Paine
All rights reserved

Printed in the United States of America

Accents Publishing
Editor: Katerina Stoykova-Klemer
Cover Photo: Patty Paine

Library of Congress Control Number: 2015948417
ISBN: 978-1-936628-37-7
First Edition

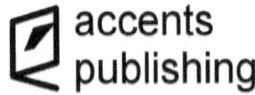

Accents Publishing is an independent press for brilliant voices. For a catalog of current and upcoming titles, please visit us on the Web at

www.accents-publishing.com

For Hayley

My gratitude beyond measure goes to everyone in the rooms.

And for Danny. May you be at peace.

# CONTENTS

## I.

Merciless / 3
O, Grief / 4
Lowering / 5
Notes on Mirrors, Already Lost / 6
Sound & Bearing / 7
September 14, 2013 / 8
What Light Does / 9
summary of the night you left / 10
Grief & Other Animals / 11
Grief Diary, Day 107 / 12
November 1, 2013 / 13
Saint of Lost Causes / 14

## II.

Erasure as Explanation / 19
my mother's last doctors visit / 22
One should not try to write after reading Levis / 24
Memorial / 25
March 15$^{th}$ / 26
Republic of Loss / 28
Pentimenti / 29
Otoliths / 30
The Talking Cure / 31

## III.

Souvenirs / 35
Prayer / 36
How Animals Grieve / 37
Limerence / 38
What You Sow / 39
Antiphony / 41
My Mother's Soup / 42
*Derecho,* 2013 / 43
July in the Desert, Doha, Qatar / 47

A Sadness Larger Than Any I Have Ever Known / 48
After a Long Time You'll Return / 49
Call and Response / 51
Closing / 52
Homing / 53

*Acknowledgments / 55*

*Biography / 57*

The first response to the disappearance of the partner consists of the anxious attempt to find him again. The goose moves about restlessly by day and night, flying great distances and visiting places where the partner might be found, uttering all the time the penetrating trisyllable long-distance call. ... The searching expeditions are extended farther and farther and quite often the searcher itself gets lost, or succumbs to an accident.... All the objective observable characteristics of the goose's behavior on losing its mate are roughly identical with human grief.

From *Grief Counseling and Grief Therapy*, J. William Worden, Ph.D., ABPP (Lorenze, 1963, quoted in Parkes, 2001, p. 44)

I.

## MERCILESS

1.

Again, the pigeons arrive,
three months, and still expecting
a scribble of seed along the sill.
How not to hate their relentless
innuendo, their inexhaustible need
to return? The hand that feeds you
is no more. Take your stupid swagger,
your useless iridescence, alight
yourselves, be gone.

2.

The night you hit the black ice
of addiction, it came to me
razor clean. After, someone wailed
and keened and turned
beggar. Someone strung
beads of *no, no, no.* Someone
collapsed, and broke open,
while someone else murmured
*over, over, over.*

*O, GRIEF*
*October 31, 2013*

Every day the white-hot
burn of you.

Grief, intransigent
bastard you, ants marching

my counters, every day I kill
you, every day you march again.

I could get used to you,
the extravagant pain of you,

the slack jawed
dead at the end

of a needle, you.
But tonight, I'll walk into you,

past Trick-or-Treaters,
with their open mouthed

bags of want, their hastily sewn
illusions. Past them,

and into you, always
into you.

## LOWERING

Leaving hour, how quick
it came. The train echoed
across the valley, over Tickfaw Creek,
trembled the ryegrass at the edge
of town, then further
still, beyond Black Mountain
clear to strange weather.
Now, six days from land
the compass has gone out of me.
These cursed waves thrash
like thieves, and what a mockery
of song the wind is making. Dearest,
the sea is another tongue
for loss, for misery, for coffin.
For grief: the rusty hinge of it,
the knife stab sudden of it.

## NOTES ON MIRRORS, ALREADY LOST

Everything after aches
river & bones &
the unsaid naming itself
endlessly. He comes to me
in dreams, and I reach
for needle & thread
to close the tear
at his knee.
This morning I found
ants in the saltshaker, a pattern
repeated in new snow
peppered with black walnuts.
I confess, with my tongue
I press His body
to the roof of my mouth,
sometimes I feel rose petal,
sometimes blister.

## SOUND & BEARING

The sea cradles me back/forth,
(what isn't
fastened, lost) I fall
back to a field of aster,
how we gorged
the scent of them.

Back to the hollow
of your neck; our hunger;
spring's long unbuttoning;
and the lightest caress
of summer in the air.

We paused
over rabbit bones (so perfect, so
small) They were
curiosity then, not omen.

SEPTEMBER 14, 2013

Unbidden, the memories come. Today, we're back in New Jersey for my mother's slow dying. The woods in the Appalachian Mountains are dense and deep, and every day we walked through them, a carpet of detritus beneath our feet. Our dog ran with an abandon so pure, so animal, part of us ran with him. One morning, we heard a rustle, first faint, then louder. We stilled, and our stillness and awareness converged. Three deer darted past, close enough to touch. After, a hush settled back into the woods, and for a moment, no one was dying, and everything was joy.

## WHAT LIGHT DOES

Today, I did nothing.
Light went on as usual

throwing leaves onto the white wall,
as if no one was watching, as if

there is no meaning in the trembling
of the leaves. Later, light moves

the leaves onto the tile floor,
and once I might have thought them

dancing, or that the shadow
of a thing is more beautiful

than the thing itself, but it's not,
it's just ordinary light, going about

its ordinary business. Now, evening is here,
and I've made it through another day

of shadows. This is not metaphor, or poetry,
it's how the unbearable

is a blade that gleams and remains
visible, long after light has gone.

## SUMMARY OF THE NIGHT YOU LEFT

vanished: two

oranges   one metronome

one earthenware ewer

left behind: a razor

wire of memory

(everything is a moment ago)

what is left

is afterimage

a bird's crop

full of pebbles.

## GRIEF & OTHER ANIMALS

His voice: slow river easing

through salt brush.

All night I dreamed of saving him,

then not,

his wrists slipping my grip

like those squirming feral kittens

born on my patio.

What madness made me

snatch them from their hissing

mother? Something inexplicable,

and black as a murder

of crows beating sky.

# GRIEF DIARY, DAY 107

*Nags Head, North Carolina, 2002:*

Everyone else boarded up
and sheltered, but we went into it,

watched waves collapse
the pier, haul it down
piece by piece. We leaned in,

felt the storm's teeth
graze our necks, let the waves

pin us to a crumbling cliff.
We needed our beauty hard,
our danger real. I was always skin

& tongue & bone—something
salvageable: an abandoned

nest; stone washed up
and pocketed. I see now,
even then, you were leaving

your body, nothing could hold you;
nothing left to save.

*Doha, Qatar, 2013:*

Today I ate a pear. Bit right
into bruise.

There is no loneliness
like mine.

Except yours.

*NOVEMBER 1, 2013*

Still, the waves, sudden
onrush of grief; a riptide
of bereft-ness. But also, a constant
undercurrent of sorrow, deeper
than solace, a tedious argument,
protracted, unresolvable.
Torture: the long hours of night.
I wake into them,
startled and jittery, my mind
electric with the thousand ways
I failed you.
I sleep for an hour, fret
for two, sleep an hour, fret
for two, until finally,
at first light, I stumble
into the day, let the dog out,
tend to the cats,
turn on NPR to stanch
the silence.
Another day, without.

## SAINT OF LOST CAUSES

Another day ellipses into night, and again
I appeal to you, O Holy Saint of Lost Causes.
Where were you when he roamed animal,
feral with hunger? Where were you
when money exchanged hands, and bag
and needle were palmed? (Of needle, I'm certain,
but was there a bag? I do not know
the language of such desperate
transactions.) I know there are too many
who are broken in this world, and I know
there will always be a man somewhere
throwing himself headlong into a machine
of his own making. But, this man, O
Holy Saint of Lost Causes, I'd give anything
for this man to be again
flesh, and bone, and breath. (And this
bargaining, even months after, you must see,
don't you, how grief is a kind of insanity?)

II.

"... the strong dead return, in poems as in our lives, and they do not come back without darkening the living."

—Harold Bloom, *Anxiety of Influence*

## ERASURE AS EXPLANATION

    mother threw herself

down       stairs,

over and over

        flew

apart inside her body.

   father slipped

         told

            nothing


    the pigeon he killed

 was a child.

Every night

     weeping and ashamed.

        she

           sees

a gleaming

    mouth gaping


   She twists,

         skin, bites

bone,     the cold

   concrete sways her

bare feet,   pain opens

       her like a wing.

\*

Night after night

        drunken cadence

never small

    enough to disappear

    never loud enough

        to be heard.

    Each morning

    the color of bruises,

        each night he descended

    screams echo

    echo

    into nothing

\*

        he lunged

teeth flashing.

For weeks,     back of cage,

constant growl.

      I soft talked him, slid

         biscuits, until he bellied close,

nuzzled my palm. That day

      at the stream you told

me you were seven

        your mother left you

             at his house every day.

You see yourself

        going back,   door opening,   muzzle

                              flash, his face

     a thousand shards.

We thought this joined us,

     we were  marked

 with the same [fucked up] brand.

I was wrong

to think suffering could hold

      us together.

      Those awful howls when he left.

## MY MOTHER'S LAST DOCTORS VISIT

paper sound
paper sound when a body
paper sound when a body lies
paper sound when a body lies back on a table
a table in a doctor's office
in the doctor's office a doctor
a doctor who is able
to do nothing

some things you never forget

like my mother
and how she turned
her head
so demure that turn of her head
when the doctor, the doctor
able to do nothing,
pressed a metal disc
to her bare chest,
her bare chest,
the turn of her
head, the lowering
of her eyes, so demure
the last time the doctor,
the doctor able to do

nothing, for the last time

listened to the murmur,

the soft, oblivious murmur

of my mother's heart

## ONE SHOULD NOT TRY TO WRITE AFTER READING LEVIS

Because it's useless, really, like trying to grasp mist
in the corner of that field, your arms pass clear
through into flailing. But there must be grace
in reaching for the ineffable, so I sit
myself back in that rented
car, our last full summer, and again
see mile after mile of corn.
And we stop once more, in the small
cemetery behind the abandoned church.
With our palms we sweep rain
plastered leaves from stone faces,
and tease stories from meager
inscriptions. Some stones are shrouded
in moss, an inscrutable velvet of possibility,
when what was possible was still
bearable. Everything was rented that summer
along the Mattaponi, its steady tide
pulling one way, then the other,
a familiar rhythm of reprieve
and relapse. Hope is the most merciful
current, seeing only the river,
not the riverbed's slow collapse.
Today, it has been four months since
your passing, and everything feels too
soon, or too late. And since I can't bear to think
of your last days, I think of my mother's,
when she'd spring from morphine haze
and say, with a sort of glee, "Still here!"
And now I find myself
saying it too: I'm still here. Still here.
Still. Here.

## MEMORIAL

It gets better, dear reader, the wailing,
I promise you, will someday break
into song. You can stand at the edge
of a river as rain stammers onto umbrellas,
and broken men read broken elegies
for another man being swept clean
down river. You can follow him down,
and believe the world is a dying
city you're ready to leave.
But, you'll remember mercy, tender
as an orchid's throat, warm
as the hand of one who loves you
on the small of your back,
and you'll return to the world. You'll stumble
down dark alleys where glass glistens
like razors, and throw yourself gracelessly
toward a flickering so faint it must be
imagined. And though everything aches,
one day you'll find yourself
dancing, and bathed in radiant light.

## MARCH 15<sup>TH</sup>

Carping, you called it,
you'd take great swallows of air, plunge

yourself into the weightless quiet
for as long as your lungs would hold.

You could never stay under
long enough. Until you could,

until you did. And now it's your birthday,
and I can't lie (though I have, I did) this day

is doing me in. It's the missing,
I suppose, and how the quiet,

the essence of it, is so thorough
when someone is never coming back.

The other night, I was watching a show
you would have liked—how long will I measure

everything by what would have
been—like measuring air against bullets ...

but anyway, in the show you would have liked,
a man is in his glass cubicle at work

when he gets a call that his lover has died.
The camera retreats, pulls us

outside the cubicle where we watch him sink,
sobbing to the floor. His co-workers in their own cubicles,

don't see or hear him, despite so much glass.
Fingers go on stabbing keyboards, phones go on

ringing, the fluorescent lights
go on lighting, which is to say, everything goes on.

And this is grief. It can take place in full transparency,
in the middle of everything, yet no one sees

or hears a thing, and everything goes on,
or doesn't, depending on which side

of the glass you're on. I want you to know
there is more hope than despair now, and

the days have been easier,
until they're not, like this day, your birthday,

a day we never made much fuss about,
but we should have.

## REPUBLIC OF LOSS

Not the animal, but its tracks
in the snow, not the wind's
slow erasure, or even the windblown leaf,
but the leaf's shadow, a mercy
between falling and fallen.
We don't get to choose
what breaks us.
In the republic of loss
bells are always ringing,
it's always winter,
and there is nothing
in our pockets.
At first light, we all bow
into the cold, hold a flicker
of light to the end
of a cigarette, inhale
an absence of language.
At night, too quiet
to hear, we whisper
a plea (some call it prayer):
*If tonight I can't sleep
in the arms of my loved one,
let me be held
in the arms of the world.*

## PENTIMENTI

All summer, I summer and shade, become
a hurt so large
I am unhoused, curbed
to a long lament.
That moment of—no matter
where I think I am, always I'm there—tragic
inattention. It's true
I looked away
for one second....
My fingers tell
me, still there:
throat and thorax.
So speak.
Say something,
say, lockstitch, or came a man
who stayed for 23 years,
say, save him, say
*I tried, I tried, I tried.*

## OTOLITHS

what is gone

                                        we bury

a satchel of words

                                        the candle's flame

words for sacred

                                        a chantey of shadows

words to make distance

                                        far from land

we pitch/roll

                                        words tumble from the nest

on our tongues

                                        the tang of salt

against rocks, our hearts

                                        (our hearts)

                *break  break  break*

## THE TALKING CURE

Sorrow, I accept you, how I'll carry you
the rest of my life. I accept

you'll sharpen yourself
endlessly. At any moment

you can drag me into your depths,
my lungs bursting with you, hours

later, still the bitter aftertaste of you.
Sorrow, you can take me, rend me

if you must, but you can't have the light
that danced leaves onto the polished

wooden floor in the room
where we sat, and I was made

clean and whole. Sorrow, take whatever
you must, but you can never take

the cure she talked into me. It is sacred,
and radiates beyond darkness & chaos & pain.

III.

## SOUVENIRS

The double function of the souvenir is to authenticate a past or otherwise remote experience and, at the same time, to discredit the present. The present is either too impersonal, too looming, or too alienating compared to the intimate and direct experience of contact which the souvenir has as its referent. This referent is authenticity. What lies between here and there is oblivion, a void marking a radical separation between past and present.

Susan Stewart, *On Longing: Narratives of the Miniature, The Gigantic, the Souvenir, the Collection* (139)

## PRAYER

O Saint of sweat
stained hats that hold
the scent of the man
I loved for so long.

Damn you.

## HOW ANIMALS GRIEVE

Today the cat who loved only you,
lay himself across my chest,
pressed his face into my neck,
and for a moment my mind went
magical, and I imagined it was you
giving what I most needed.
I held him, my tears
wet his fur, and though
first, the water truck rattled by,
then children shrieked past, startling
things that would normally
send him running,
he never moved,
or opened his eyes.
He burrowed into me
offering his warmth
and his weight, and I held him,
for as long as I could.

## LIMERENCE
### for Jim

You, a dream I wake from,
the few minutes I believe
it's real, and all the moments
after, when it's not. You
the kiss I turned from, and each
stone in my cathedral of regret.
You the hero rushing into a burning
building. Hours later the smoldering
embers, still you. You an escape
folded into suitcases and hidden
under a marriage bed.

## WHAT YOU SOW

The orchid died
from long absence,

but the avocado you planted
from seed, mere stalk, bereft

of leaves when we left,
blossomed like a memory

of the avocado tree you grew
a decade ago. You started it

with toothpicks in a tumbler
of tap water, waited

for its spidery roots, plunged
your calloused hands into clean

soil, planted and re-planted
as it grew and grew,

its canopy of green
scraping the ceiling,

until finally it could grow
no more, and it grew

root bound, slowly
withered, and died. I will try

to keep this fledgling
echo of the past alive, this thing

that grew in neglect,
I will try not to kill

with love. Each time
I water it, I think of your hands

making a hollow
for the seed, your hope

that the past could be undone
in the future. I envy this

tenacious plant because it knows
nothing of sorrow,

how it unpetals a person,
brutal, like scissors, but slower,

like how the O in widow
unfurls into moan …

## ANTIPHONY

Go back to that stream, touch
your lips to the cold, clear quivering,
draw into yourself a time when it was simple
as this to be quenched, to draw in what was
needed. Walk back over the dewed grass
of your past, past the water tower you filled
with dark imaginings, feel
the air crisp & clean on your skin, call
this hope, and carry it
to these moments when a photograph
can send you spiraling, your husband
now six months gone, waiting at the bottom
of an escalator in some airport
or another, everyone hurrying to be somewhere
else, except for this one man, waiting
for you to descend. How a face can be
indelible, yet fade so quickly, is an alchemy
best left unknowable. Hold that sting
of hope, and call out
the name of one who ministered
to you, over & over, until from the dark
you hear your own name return
to you, wild, and rising and clear.

## MY MOTHER'S SOUP

Hours packing artifacts—
a bowl of doll heads, lacquered box
of wishbones, bundles of shark
cartilage that claim
to heal—the whole time I crave
the soup you made the last time
I saw you. I tear escarole,
dice scallions, cube tofu
and taro, and toss it in stock dark
with anchovy. The kitchen fills
with apparitions of steam,
and the smell of damp earth.
I turn up the heat, desperate
to quench this hunger, so raw, so large.

## DERECHO, *2013*

Name it:    mirage    or    summer:    a torn

       hawk's wing nailed to a silvered

       shack buckled and coughing alfalfa

       we toss to the donkeys who will eat as much as we give,

       jaws working    working    working

       long after everything is gone their lips go on

       nuzzling damp earth.

Once,

there was a boy & a girl, and when they joined

hands everything broken was mirrored & doubled.

(This can not end

                 happily, of course.)

Crown, pail, broke, endless tumbling, everything always too hot, or too cold, all the houses blew down, the frog stayed frog, the dead brawled and quarreled, there was no trail of breadcrumbs, and Cinderella would have given anything to unfit that stupid slipper.

Begin again.

Name it    half-brother    or    stepfather

       he who forever altered the trajectory of

             brother/daughter

>is one way of saying it. He who planted that sliver
>of shame (o, how it tore and tore for years and years)
>>is another.

>>Once there was a boy & a girl, unmothered
>>and hollow as Cicada shells. You must see,
>>dear reader, this story can not end
>>happily.

Begin again.

Some days it comes like this, fragmented
and untidy.

>Persist.
>Persist.
>Persist.

>You have to believe that language is a body
>that won't die.

Fragments …

In the house of mourning every room is a cage.
Each day something nameless:

how the scent of a man lingers:

how shirts in a closet become haunted:

how their useless empty

sleeves hold nothing

but rage.


Do you remember the sky before the storm?

Its irreal glow, how the wind stole

our clothes from the line, and you

chased, laughing?


Later, long after

the electricity quit, we lay in bed holding

hands, and listened to the rain

and wind

do awful things (*Derecho,* they called it.)

Branches fell gunshot onto the tin roof,

but the boy wasn't afraid. Even as the house heaved

and trembled, even when windows broke,

and doors burst open.

The boy wasn't afraid.

The girl was.

The girl was always afraid.

*

But look, the sun has risen again

into mantra: grief humbles,

grief softens,

it makes one more

kind.

It must.

It must.

It must.

## *JULY IN THE DESERT, DOHA, QATAR*

Though this July I am gone,

there have been many July's in the desert,

and I know feral dogs are stalking

the acacia's meager shade.

Their muzzles fly stippled and twitching,

I know they are dreaming

kind touch, despite such thick-fisted

heat, even the bulbuls panting.

A desert is a hundred shades

of brown, an open mouth

thirst. It teaches your body

doesn't belong

to you, it belongs to the wind,

to the voice, even from afar,

it's in my ear. I know when I return

I'll do as it says,

I'll lie, simply lie, weeping

on the shimmering, seductive sand.

## *A SADNESS LARGER THAN ANY I HAVE EVER KNOWN*

Just over a year, and still moments I don't want
to do this anymore, I don't know how
to say it another, more poetic, way.
But, I get up, (*stay on your feet, stay
on your feet* ...) and I hold
the sheets straight from the dryer,
and that I still care about warm
and clean, gives me a kind of hope.
Rilke, though you comfort me, I am not a young
poet, not a young anything, but I want
to believe something is happening
within me, that the world
won't let me fall.

## *AFTER A LONG TIME YOU'LL RETURN*

after a long time you'll return
to the place you grew up
grew into
grew away from
grew tired of
grew angry with
grew strong because
the place where you grew afraid
then grew larger
than your fears
you'll go back
and when Route 517 crests
and the mountains appear
there will be no words
for such beauty
and you'll cry
you will
when you return
to the place you grew up
you'll go to your high school
and stand on the practice field
see flutes trumpets clarinets
lying in the grass
hear a bass drum beat and fall
into long ago half time routines
kicking up crickets
just like when you didn't know nostalgia
would grow with you
or that some names
would come untied
that you'd lose
the taste of apples

from the orchard behind the track
or that certain moments would grow huge
over the years like that
night you stole
swallows of your stepfather's rot-gut
went to the school dance and were driven
home by someone whose name
didn't come untied will never
come untied and you
sat in his Firebird
the air charged his hand
in your hand a soft
murmur of voices
while trees glistened
with snow melt
and you hadn't left
or grown old
or learned how fast
a moment can pass
how desperately
you'd want it back

## CALL AND RESPONSE

All through our last year we find remnants,
the shell of a turtle long after what lived

turned dust, the skull of a fox, clean
as the first scent of fall, a nest untangling

in the wind, the same wind that rouses
the chimes, sweeps dead leaves

into the river, and farther
down river a man hauls a net

into his boat, the way you hauled secrets
into yourself, each day growing

heavier and heavier. This morning,
I sat on the patio crying for you,

and I heard my neighbor teaching
his toddler to count. He called out each

number, and she chimed back her bird-
like approximations. And though I've never

met them, I loved them, and for today,
this was enough.

CLOSING
*Thursday October 3rd, 2013*

 *To Hayley, who changed my mind.*

In my confused and stricken state,
when my mouth was a mausoleum
of regret, you sat with me.

When the dog of shame paced
and frothed, you met its rabid gaze,
and you sat with me.

After death, that final crowning
act, when nearly everything died,
you sat with me.

On a damp bench, close to the edge
of the river, while grief lapped
relentlessly, you sat with me.

And because you sat with me,
this morning, an apparition of mist rose
over the mountains, the river held
the face of the sky, leaves blazed
with light, and everything burned
with beauty.

## HOMING
### For Law

What can we do but love
ourselves out of darkness.
Out of the past shrouded
in smoke. Have mercy
on our one, imperfect heart.
Ah, heart, you homing
pigeon, ink mark on bronze,
bless you, your relentless
returning. The whole time
while I grieved, and grieved
and grieved, like thunder,
far off, you were calling to me,
so quietly, I almost missed you
for the weeping.

## ACKNOWLEDGMENTS

Grateful acknowledgment to the editors of the following publications in which some of these poems have appeared:

"Lowering," *Anti-*

"What You Sow" and "What Light Does," *Blackbird: A Journal of Literature and the Arts*

"O, Grief," *Georgetown Review*

"Notes on Mirrors, Already Lost," *OCHO*

"Merciless" and "One should not try to write after reading Levis," *Revolution House*

"Antiphony," *THRUSH,* May 2015

"Call & Response," *The Adroit Journal,* Fall 2015

"Grief Diary, Day 107" and "Saint of Lost Causes," *The Louisville Review*

Thank you to Dan Nowak of Imaginary Friend Press, who published the chapbook *Feral,* where some of these poems first appeared.

# BIOGRAPHY

Patty Paine is the author of *The Sounding Machine* (Accents Publishing), *Feral* (Imaginary Friend Press), *Elegy & Collapse* (Finishing Line Press), and co-editor of *Gathering the Tide: An Anthology of Contemporary Arabian Gulf Poetry* (Garnet Publishing & Ithaca Press) and *The Donkey Lady and Other Tales from the Arabian Gulf* (Berkshire). Her poems, reviews, and interviews have appeared in *Blackbird, The Louisville Review, Gulf Stream, The Journal* and other publications. She is the founding editor of *Diode Poetry Journal* and *Diode Editions,* and is an assistant professor of English at Virginia Commonwealth University Qatar where she teaches writing and literature, and is interim director of Liberal Arts & Sciences.

www.ingramcontent.com/pod-product-compliance
Lightning Source LLC
Chambersburg PA
CBHW021451080526
44588CB00009B/802